DIMENSIONS OF HEALTH

PUBLIC HEALTH

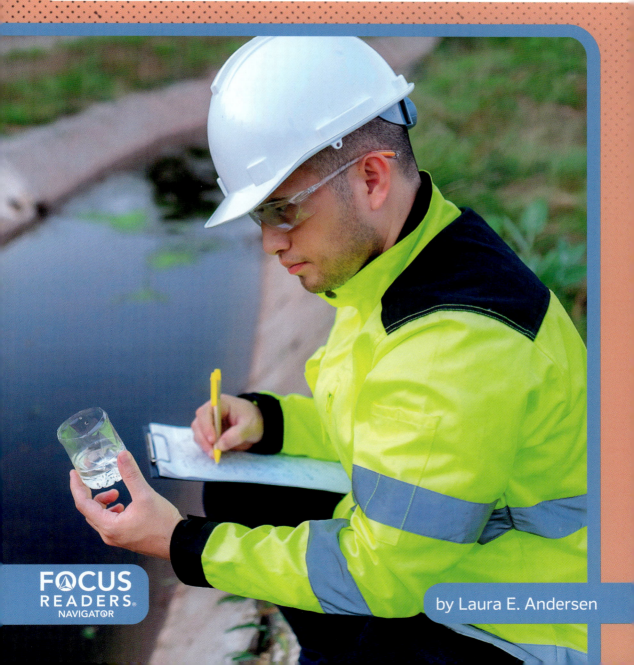

by Laura E. Andersen

WWW.FOCUSREADERS.COM

Copyright © 2026 by Focus Readers®, Mendota Heights, MN 55120. All rights reserved. No part of this book may be reproduced or utilized in any form or by any means without written permission from the publisher.

Focus Readers is distributed by North Star Editions:
sales@northstareditions.com | 888-417-0195

Produced for Focus Readers by Red Line Editorial.

Photographs ©: Shutterstock Images, cover, 1, 4–5, 7, 8–9, 11, 13, 14–15, 17, 19, 20–21, 22, 26–27, 29; Red Line Editorial, 23; Paula Bronstein/Getty Images News/Getty Images, 24

Library of Congress Cataloging-in-Publication Data
Library of Congress Cataloging-in-Publication Data is available on the Library of Congress website.

ISBN
979-8-88998-527-3 (hardcover)
979-8-88998-587-7 (ebook pdf)
979-8-88998-559-4 (hosted ebook)

Printed in the United States of America
Mankato, MN
082025

ABOUT THE AUTHOR
Laura E. Andersen helped lead a local public health response to COVID-19 in Saint Paul, Minnesota. She also worked at the Minnesota Department of Health and the State of Alaska Division of Public Health. She has a master's degree in public health from the University of Minnesota.

TABLE OF CONTENTS

CHAPTER 1
Clinic Visit 5

CHAPTER 2
What Is Public Health? 9

CHAPTER 3
Many Levels 15

CONNECTIONS
Avoiding Outbreaks 18

CHAPTER 4
A Group Effort 21

CHAPTER 5
How to Help 27

Focus Questions • 30
Glossary • 31
To Learn More • 32
Index • 32

CHAPTER 1

CLINIC VISIT

It is October 2020. A boy comes home from school feeling sick. His mom thinks he might have COVID-19. So, she takes him to a drive-through clinic to get tested. There, the boy and his mom join a line of cars. After a few minutes, they drive up to a health worker. She wears a mask, gloves, and a plastic apron.

In the early 2020s, some clinics offered free testing for COVID-19.

5

The boy rolls down his window. The worker holds a long cotton swab. She explains that she will twirl it in each of his nostrils. At first, the boy feels nervous. But the worker is smiling with her eyes. She tests his mom, too. She gets a new swab. And she repeats the explanation in Spanish, which the boy's mom speaks.

GLOBAL CRISIS

The COVID-19 virus spread around the world in the early 2020s. Millions of people got sick. Hospitals struggled to treat everyone. Public health workers tried to slow the spread. They helped people get tests to know if they were **contagious**. And they told people ways to avoid spreading germs.

COVID-19 mainly spread when people breathed the virus in or out. To help prevent this, people wore masks.

The worker takes both swabs. She says they will get a call in a few days with their test results. If they are sick and need to stay home, another worker will help them get medicine.

7

CHAPTER 2

WHAT IS PUBLIC HEALTH?

Some types of health are about one person. But public health focuses on large groups of people. It measures how healthy a community is. And it tries to improve the whole group's health.

The groups that public health looks at vary in size. A group might be one part of a city. Or it could be an entire country.

Public health workers may use signs to show people ways to stay healthy.

Public health workers collect details about the people in the group. They look for trends or patterns. They try to understand the group's health as a whole.

A group's health depends on many things. It is shaped by physical, mental, and environmental factors. Physical factors have to do with people's bodies. They include things like diseases or fitness levels. Mental health focuses on people's thoughts, feelings, and behavior. Environmental factors have to do with where people live. Social factors affect health, too. These include things like what color someone's skin is or how much money a person has.

People who live close to factories or chemical plants have higher rates of certain diseases.

Public health looks at how these factors affect communities. It studies why some groups are healthier than others. Access to resources often plays a role. For example, people who live in places without clean water are more likely to get sick. But people who regularly visit doctors tend to stay healthy. That's partly because doctors can find and treat problems. It's also because doctors teach people how to take care of themselves. In fact, education is another resource that helps people stay healthy.

Public health workers identify communities with poor health or few resources. Then they try to help. For

MANY IMPACTS

Different health factors often work together. For example, it's important to have friends or family to talk to. This improves people's mental health. But that's not all. When people feel supported, their physical health tends to be better, too. Sometimes, one factor can have many impacts. For example, **pollution** is an environmental factor. Living near dirty air or water increases people's risk for many diseases.

Workers in Indonesia hold an event teaching ways to improve the health of women and babies.

instance, workers may build toilets in **rural** areas. That makes diseases less likely to spread through people's waste. Or workers may teach parents good ways to feed and take care of kids. They may also deliver food or supplies to people's homes.

Home / Newsroom / Fact sheets / Det...
Zika virus

Zika virus

CHAPTER 3

MANY LEVELS

Some types of public health workers treat diseases. However, public health focuses mostly on preventing problems. So, workers often help people find care and information.

One of the biggest public health groups is the World Health Organization (WHO). The WHO is run by the United Nations.

The World Health Organization (WHO) website provides facts about a variety of health problems.

It does studies and leads programs around the world. It helps people learn where and when diseases are spreading. And it explains how to stay safe.

Most countries have a health department as part of their government. It provides care and services to people who live there. The United States has the Department of Health and Human Services (HHS). HHS manages many programs. One is Medicaid. It provides **health insurance** to low-income families.

HHS also runs the Centers for Disease Control and Prevention (CDC). The CDC studies illnesses. It shares information with the public. Its website has facts

The Centers for Disease Control and Prevention (CDC) is based in Atlanta, Georgia. It also has labs and offices around the world.

about diseases and ways to stop their spread.

Each US state runs its own health department as well. So do many counties and cities. These local groups often work directly with residents. They may help residents get **vaccines**. Or they may provide healthy food for people in need.

> CONNECTIONS

AVOIDING OUTBREAKS

Epidemiologists are one type of public health worker. They study diseases and how they spread. To do this, they track the types and cases of illness in an area. Often, this area is a state. But it could also be a city, a county, or an entire country.

Epidemiologists try to prevent outbreaks. These are times when diseases start spreading quickly. To prevent this, health care workers often team up. For example, suppose several students at a school have measles. An epidemiologist might call the school nurse. The nurse could offer vaccines to students who need them. A health educator might visit the school. He could help families understand how to stay healthy.

Some diseases spread easily. Doctors must tell local health departments when they learn

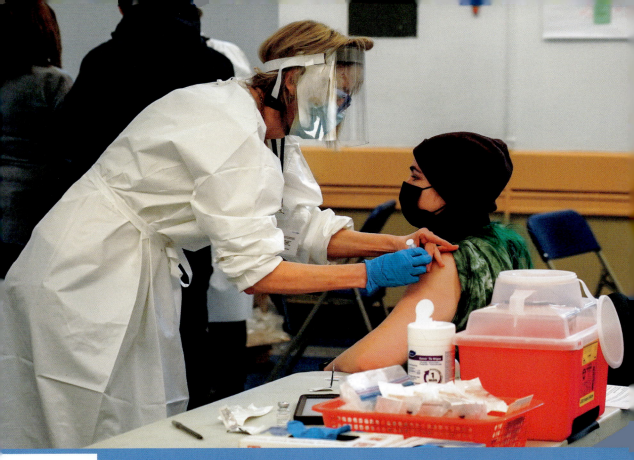

When fewer people get vaccines for contagious diseases, such as COVID-19 or measles, outbreaks become more likely.

of cases. Then department workers can try to keep other people from getting sick. Workers may contact people who live or work with a sick person. They may ask if those people feel unwell. Other workers may visit sick people's homes. They may bring food or medicine so the people can stay home.

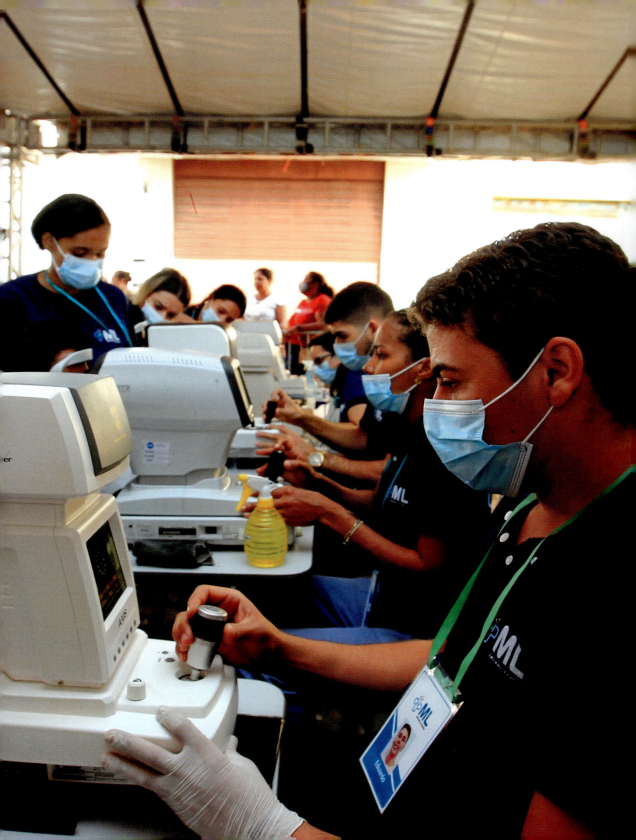

CHAPTER 4

A GROUP EFFORT

Public health departments work to identify what problems their communities face. Then they create plans. They look for changes that might improve people's health.

Public health is complex. So, one plan often has many steps. For example, suppose a town wants to improve kids'

Some places have few doctors or clinics. Public health workers may visit to provide care.

Food plays a key role in people's health. So, some programs help people get fresh groceries.

health. The town might build playgrounds to help kids stay active. Schools might start programs that provide healthy lunches during the summer. Local leaders might help run a **mentoring** group that gives kids support and advice.

The people in a community are likely to know what will work best there. So, departments often team up with them to make plans. They ask community members to identify problems. And they ask what changes they think would help.

For example, one health department studied three counties in Wisconsin. It learned that many people there felt depressed. Health workers talked to

AREAS OF CARE

Health departments work on a variety of issues.

 VACCINES

 FOOD SAFETY

 INFECTIOUS DISEASES

 CHRONIC DISEASES

 INJURIES AND VIOLENCE

 PROTECTING THE ENVIRONMENT

 BABIES AND PREGNANCY

 PREPARING FOR EMERGENCIES

 LIMITING TOBACCO USE

Malaria is a serious problem in many countries. Health workers track the disease and try to help decrease the number of cases.

community members. They found that many people struggled to access mental health care. They also learned some reasons why. Lack of transportation and long wait lists were two reasons.

Health workers also study if plans are working. They often use surveys. They might call people and ask questions. Or they might collect **data** about people's health. They compare recent information to details from the past. This shows what, if anything, has changed. Workers may visit communities, too. They ask for people's opinions about plans or services. If people identify problems, workers can think of ways to address them.

NEW VACCINES

Some public health workers do research. They look for new ways to solve problems. Kizzmekia Corbett-Helaire is one researcher. She studies diseases. During the COVID-19 **pandemic**, she worked at the National Institutes of Health (NIH). The NIH is a part of HHS that looks for new treatments. Corbett-Helaire and her team developed a vaccine that protected against the COVID-19 virus. It saved millions of lives.

CHAPTER 5

HOW TO HELP

Even though public health is about groups, individuals can support it. One way is by volunteering. At some public health clinics, volunteers provide medical care or testing. But there are many ways to help. People can help with fundraising or planning. Or they can serve as **translators**.

Schools and communities can host blood drives. At these events, people donate blood for clinics or hospitals to use.

People can also support laws that promote public health. For example, some laws require students to get vaccines before starting school. Vaccines help prevent serious illnesses from spreading. Other laws reduce pollution. They may ban burning trash. Or they may start

TROUBLE IN FLINT

In 2014, people in Flint, Michigan, noticed changes in the city's water. It smelled bad. And it was brown. People asked local leaders for help. At first, leaders ignored them. But people continued to speak up. Eventually, the problem made national news. Scientists found that the water had dangerous levels of lead and bacteria. Public health workers helped people get filters and testing kits.

Many people in Flint, Michigan, relied on bottled water for drinking, cooking, and washing things during the years that the city's water was unsafe.

programs for **composting** or recycling. People can support these laws. And they can tell others about them.

Kids can work together to start programs at their schools. They can call for less waste or healthier food. All these actions help communities become cleaner, safer, and healthier.

29

FOCUS QUESTIONS

Write your answers on a separate piece of paper.

1. Write a paragraph that explains the main ideas of Chapter 2.

2. Do you think it's more helpful to treat diseases or prevent them? Why?

3. What type of work does an epidemiologist do?
    - **A.** study diseases and how they spread
    - **B.** plan ways for cities to increase people's health
    - **C.** take care of sick students at a school

4. Which of these would be an environmental factor?
    - **A.** how many factories are near a neighborhood
    - **B.** how many close friends a person has
    - **C.** how much sugar a person eats each day

Answer key on page 32.

GLOSSARY

composting
The process of breaking down food and other organic material, often to turn it into fertilizer.

contagious
Able to spread a sickness to other people.

data
Information collected to study or track something.

health insurance
A program that helps pay for people's health care.

mentoring
Helping people learn and grow, often by pairing them with someone older or more experienced.

pandemic
A disease that spreads quickly around the world.

pollution
Harmful substances that collect in the air, water, or soil.

rural
Having few cities, towns, or people.

translators
People who change words from one language to another.

vaccines
Substances that help prevent people from getting certain diseases.

TO LEARN MORE

BOOKS

Dalal, Anita. *Improving Health: Women Who Led the Way.* Children's Press, 2022.

Lilley, Matt. *Detecting Infectious Disease.* Focus Readers, 2024.

Miller, Marie-Therese, PhD. *Jobs in Health Care.* Abdo Publishing, 2024.

NOTE TO EDUCATORS

Visit **www.focusreaders.com** to find lesson plans, activities, links, and other resources related to this title.

INDEX

Centers for Disease Control and Prevention (CDC), 16
clinics, 5, 27
communities, 9, 11–12, 21–25, 29
composting, 29
COVID-19, 5–6, 25

data, 24
diseases, 10, 12–13, 15–17, 18, 23, 25

environmental factors, 10, 12

epidemiologists, 18

Flint, Michigan, 28

health departments, 16–17, 18–19, 21–23
health insurance, 16

illnesses, 16, 18, 28

Medicaid, 16
mental health, 10, 12, 24

physical factors, 10, 12
pollution, 12, 28

resources, 11–12
rural, 13

social factors, 10

translators, 27

vaccines, 17, 18, 23, 25, 28

World Health Organization (WHO), 15

Answer Key: 1. Answers will vary; 2. Answers will vary; 3. A; 4. A